Can I Finish, Please?

Also by Catherine Bowman

The Plath Cabinet
Notarikon
Rock Farm
1-800-HOT-RIBS

as editor

Word of Mouth: Poems Featured on NPR's All Things Considered

Can I Finish, Please?

Catherine Bowman

Four Way Books
Tribeca

Please direct all inquiries to:
Editorial Office
Four Way Books
POB 535, Village Station
New York, NY 10014
www.fourwaybooks.com

Library of Congress Cataloging-in-Publication Data

Bowman, Catherine.
[Poems. Selections]
Can I finish, please? / Catherine Bowman.
pages ; cm
ISBN 978-1-935536-66-6 (pbk. : alk. paper)
I. Title.
PS3552.O87555A6 2016
811'.54--dc23

2015028571

This book is manufactured in the United States of America and printed on acid-free paper.

Four Way Books is a not-for-profit literary press. We are grateful for the assistance
we receive from individual donors, public arts agencies, and private foundations.

This publication is made possible with public funds from the New York State Council on the Arts,
a state agency.

[clmp]

We are a proud member of the Community of Literary Magazines and Presses.

Distributed by University Press of New England
One Court Street, Lebanon, NH 03766

To B.J.O.

Contents

III

Beginner,
Perpetual beginner. . .

—Theodore Roethke

Dedication

For the musk rose's curved thorns

    and pans of pinto beans on the stove,

for the cursed green-handled knife,

    for all cursed knives, this binding-rope splitter

unfurling alfalfa and orchard grass song,

    for your left hand, angler, those three middle fingers,

a Gull's Hornbook, spelling guide

    for beginners, for your mouth ocean,

sometimes out of work, always busy,

    for your never-has-been, for your always-will-be,

to the memory of the running lights of firefly squid,

    for the running lights of all fish lanterns with barbed chins,

in deepest darkest waters—chemical glitter, floating

    through tidal pools, tickled by sea grass,

for this grotto, the phlox, for the rabbit

I carried in a cage blindfolded in a dream

trying to hail a taxi, for all formidable flowers,

    wild ancient apple trees,

for the massive knead and plump of frog song in summer,

    for the heat of the skunk cabbage and frog lily,

for the body manifold, the marigold in spring, for clover,

    for fat tomatoes,

for goldenrods and the beet and poinsettia,

    for the stars that guide night migrants,

the catbirds, thrushes, thrashers, wood warblers

    and owls, ducks and indigo buntings over cornfields,

for the 100 million songbirds and shorebirds,

    guided by ocean winds, their flyways,

for the inner-sun compass and the North Star compass,

    for the mammoth sunflower, for home,

for the drowsy opening and closing of flowers,

for the swallows wound up in a heap,

sleeping all winter in the low beds of a river,

to their long winter sleep, for bees sunk deep

in honey, for the frogs now sleeping in mud,

for the giant sequoia with three acres of roots,

for you lost wine, lost skin—

for you new wine, new skin—

for the lungfish, he lives without moving,

for you ash pit, foraging for lost nails

and old wire on the last day of summer,

for the breath of horses eating hay in winter,

in memory of the source unknown

and before gods did fight, for clouds,

to you nothing and to you everything,

to your ordinary ocean that I distill

nightly without interruption,

    for the mourning doves in the vine behind the house,

to you desert road, the path behind our heart,

    where you walk with the lion,

to him, to the river, never ending,

    you keep going.

I

Stalker, a Ghost Flower

I pressed my lips to the foreskin
of the windowpane, fruit-wet
with a night delivery of cloud
from a forgotten ocean prowling
over the fields, here to the garden,
turning weeds into a distillery
of secrets at dawn before the cure
of French roast and you still asleep,
inside, in feathers. I wiped my lips
of the pre-June with the back of my
hand, swallowed hard, renewed
myself: my fingers smelled
of the lowland where I unfurled
and flailed and spun in the wind
like a torn French filmstrip.
I kissed the pane again and again—
did you know I was out there,
locked out? This glazed transparency
I kissed, the cool pleasure of contact
to my lips, so thirsty, blessed
dew, how the impression of lips
disappeared, my reflection
so uncut it could have been my brother's.
Lips on glass—gentle—sometimes
I kiss metal—like a dog licking
an old fire poker, craving mineral.
Once I kissed the mouth of a revolver
to see how it felt. Kissed rocks
from the bottom of the ocean, ate

red clay—as a child at the edge
of the desert I lived one summer
on wild berries and rose petals
carpeting the driveway across the street.
I was hungry. The beasting: the lamb's
first taste, a mix of milk and blood.
My mouth, a lambing, a haven.
I will not harm you. Like lightning,
I need an element between you and me.

Makeshift

From two pieces of string and oil-fattened feathers he made a father.
She made a mother from loss buttons and ocean debris.

Lacking a grave, they embottled themselves
in a favorite liqueur, the pyx and plethora of clouds.

With the heart stripped and clear-cut, they rekindled the stars,
created a glossary of seeds.

Down the fire ladder, rung after fiery rung, they gather, salvage,
fiddle about, curse and root, laugh themselves silly,

en masse assemble a makeshift holy city. In the holy city,
makeshift, they assemble en masse, silly themselves,

laugh and root, curse the fiddle, gather salvage rung
after fiery rung as they ladder their fire down.

A glossary seeded creates stars, strips clear the diamond-cut heart.

They sold clouds, the plethora and pyx of liqueur. Favored themselves
embottled in grave lack, ocean debris and loss buttons,

where Mother made a father who made feathers
from fattened oil and string pieces for two.

For the Lost Children of San Pedro Sula

With nighttime rubbed
into your pathways,
you traversed never,

not quite and always,
your resins pressed
and seasoned with what

was taken away, no longer
present, ever present
out of sight, neither here

nor there. You traveled
through the vanquished,
the long lost, the no place

within us, without us,
through river beds, beyond
forests, over cities and plains.

Wrapped in wind and clouds
and rains, the departed,
the disappeared, the absconded,

you wandered, careful not to trample
on small creatures or wake demons,
hand in hand, far off and at close range.

Blue Egg

A woman makes an eye
in a hollow egg with the tip
of a needle and then gazes
through the egg holding
a girl faraway in her vision.
The girl alone among an oracular
thicket of alders marvels
over a blue egg in a nest
made of bark, tree moss, and lichen.
She holds the egg to her eye
and beholds herself faraway, enclosed
in a ship's hold, a windowless prison.
Above her the stars pour down
from the vault of heaven, the firmament's
syrup over a cargo of smuggled humans.
The boiler man below sings of Pluto's
black doors. He holds up a black egg
to the night and sees a bird rise up
from an egg-shaped burial ground
for kings. The bird flies far and wide
through time to a man who drives
to work listening to books on tape.
This week it's Einstein and he's trying
to get his head around infinity, how
there is no such thing, how we're just
one giant, great egg-shaped sphere
and beyond that there's nothing.
Just that morning over eggs, gazing
outside at the perpetual blue

heron spreading his wings, watching
over the oval pond he guards,
the translucent berries, the roses,
the soak in the cedar-lined tub,
wondering if what he sees above
is a star or a planet. While, faraway,
a girl makes an eye in the hollow egg
and then gazes through the egg
holding herself, a woman in her
vision. *Child, it's not hard to descend;*
coming back is what's difficult,
the woman whispers. Then carefully,
she begins to grind the spices,
five varieties, the cure, the broth,
the long process of stirring. *Ghost ships*
always travel against the wind, she whispers,
not really knowing why and to no one really.

Wave

We will miss
most the sea:

the swell
of the ride

in the bell's
great pull

that undoes us,
makes us

unfinished
sky mirror—

our exit
a violence

we endure,
dive under,

feel the seam
break over

the moon,
our backs.

The Sink

She loves to talk on the phone
while washing the dinner dishes,
catching up long distance or
dealing with issues closer to home,
the reconnoitring with the long lost
or a recent so-and-so. She finds it
therapeutic, washing down
the aftermath. And that feeling
she gets in her stomach with a loved one's
prolonged silence. And under the sink
in the dark among the L-pipes, the confederate
socket wrenches, lost twine, wire lei,
sink funk, steel-wool lemnisci, leitmotifs
of oily sacraments, a broken compass forever
pointing southeast by east, mold codices,
ring-tailed dust motes from days well served,
a fish-shaped flyswatter with blue horns,
fermented lemures, fiery spectres,
embottled spirit vapors swirling in the crude
next to the Soft Scrub, the vinegared
and leistered sealed in tins, delicious with saltines,
gleaned spikelets, used-up votives. . . .
In the back in the corner forgotten
an old coffee can of bacon fat
from a month of sinful Sundays,
a luna moth embossed, rising—a morning star.

Provisional

When he procured her,
      she purveyed him.
            When he rationed her out,

she made him provisional.
      On being provisional,
            he made her trough.

On being trough,
      she made him silo.
            Now once a silo,

he made her feed.
      On being fed,
            she made him utensil.

On being utensil,
      he turned her downhill.
            So being downhill,

she made him skis.
      When she was stethoscope,
            he was her steady beat.

From beat she was dog,
      from dog he was fetch,
            from fetch she was jab,

from jab he was fake.
        When he was complex
                equation, she was simple math.

So she made him strong
        evidence, accessory after the fact.
           So he turned her eyes

private, made her man
        on the lam. When he became aesthete,
            she became a claw-foot bath.

So she made him rudimentary
        fault lines; so he made her volcanic rim.
              So she made him an unruly quorum;

so he made her party whip.
        That's when they both became unholy
           mirror, and then both became lips.

From lips they were trumpet,
        from trumpet they were mute.
           From mute, stride piano;

from stride, left-hand bass notes.
        That's when they both became psalm,
           each other's scrubby tract.

The Hold

I remember the first time
he held me, our harmonics,
our to-and-fro—I felt
more embowered
than embraced—a mouthpiece
to a wind instrument
in my pocket, a song
in my head, a calyx
maintaining a grip,
arched or curved,
recessed like a bow, bent.

*

There is a lake in Peru
where at dusk a giant lily
rises up to the surface,
opens, releases a citrus
scent the beetles
cannot resist. They alight
on the central petals,
the lily closes, sinks back
down to the depths,
all night underwater
the gorging drone
of beetles rolling
in the belly of the giant
lily, later released,
groggy, pollen-soaked, bent,
bowing back into the night.

Beds

This narrow holster
        he slips you into,
                calibrates and recalibrates

you, a new-minted rifle.
        This placeholder,
                where you zero

each other over and over,
        until neither
                man or woman,

now an amalgamation
        of animals, a private
                zodiac on the sheets.

This ark. This cipher.
        This hole. This palatial nest
                of burning birds. Of roses. Of thorns.

This hunting ground
        you carry on your back.
                This good dog at your feet.

This road stuffed with horsehair
        and little hurts, secrets
                and loose change.

This road where you walk,
  eyes shut, arms wide open
    or crossed at the chest

as you follow him each night
  through the blue threshold,
    off the edge of a cliff.

*

This cradle floating high
  in the ether,
    this nursery of altars

with forepaws tethered
  to the heart.
    All potential.

Rocking in this idiot box,
  bathed in yellow.
    Egg cup.

This plate
  where you sip
    a vial of his song.

*

Now, this bed,
        this conjuror's table
                made from williwaw

and doldrums, foam scud,
        the flammable, burnished
                with agate eye, cloud-wrapped,

cloud-bedeviled.
        This con act
                where you cut each

other in half,
        invent alphabets.
                This bag of tricks.

This disappearing act.
        This mistaken bed,
                wrong couch, errata

mattress, sack
        of false moves,
                omission dock. Forged

levee. This lavish mandala.
        This empty lot. This salt
                flat where you trade

22

horses after a long day
       at the track. This bed
              of bitterroot, harebell,

twin flower, moss rose,
       motherwort, phlox. . .
              This parlor where you lie,

embossed through
       the curtains:
              a moon tattoo.

This trench that you dig
       with your very
              own shovel. This tongue,

this conduit, where
       he fashions himself
              an electrobiologist,

this power grid
       where he ignites your sun—
              this gift

of tongues. This silence
       you heal him with.
              This candlelit pasture,

this jewel box,
        this night boat.
                This silver sycamore

by the bedroom window,
        where vultures, robed
                and appointed, chuff,

imitate the wind, observe
        each other in the solemn
                work of eating the animal

half of the animal.
        This primal throne
                where you lounge,

wane and wax, sprawl,
        puff on cigars, slay
                yourselves, admit curiosity,

grovel and prophesize,
        heave and hove, tie each other
                into a paradise

of aloe and knots, follow
        his path of opposites.
                This road where

he takes you,
        where you take him—
                posthaste, wound in sheets—

to hell and back to heaven. This river
        where you gather
                his body parts,

where he puts you back
        together. Where you have faith
                that you control

every weather as you
        give up your cattle
                to a forgotten sky god.

        *

This opening wedge
        bedizened
                in unmentionables.

This evangelical mirror
        severed from a cold calendar.
                This life sentence

25

tucked under the pillow.
        Refracting table. Cleft.
                Fissure. Chasm. Gorge.

This peephole. This lifeboat.
        This tented field.
            Aperture.

Staked by a lunar vendetta,
        bare-ankled, bare-chested,
                bare-throated, unshod,

bare-backed,
        this breeding ground,
            this Venus spread,

this birthing rack
        you die into each night.
        This job.

This hatchery.
        This giant cypress,
            a rookery for tears,

for joy. This forcing bed
        for hard labor, playtime,
            the work of dreams.

Bed of geraniums and lily
        and owls, proud owls.
                Where you are always called back—

this wallow of red clover
        to foal and cast
                out spirits.

This urine- and rose-soaked
        heptacord. This seawall
                for the mother

of all-consuming storms.
        This sweet hereafter
                where you fatten

each other up, luxuriate,
        bite off more
                than you can chew.

This auditory apparatus.
        This ear. This wizen for grief.
        This bulrush

for laughter and song.
        On the seashores of Lindisfarne
                Lindisfarne oyster beds.

*

27

This wind door,
        rough-hewn
                and hammered out,

hornbook, typhoon,
        bull-necked, chiseled.
                This bulk. This pulpit.

This lamb.
        This archive
                of your sound bites

and inklings and whispers.
        Logged and indexed
                account book and ledger

where he tabulates your minutes,
        where you balance
                his score. Enscrolled in gold

and yellow, your upper
        and lower case
                in this book of hours.

This calculus of belief
        you form on the threads.
                Torn for life. Knocked full.

*

This magma of bullion
        and ruby
                rising up—this orb

at dawn, this father confessor.
        This fat church
                enshrined and enrobed,

wearing nothing
        but seven-league boots,
                you give in to seven sacraments,

summon all matter
        of spirits from vinegar
                to comb honey,

count blessings
        on a headboard,
                renounce common courtesies

or courteously revel
        in each other's
                often-told stories,

plot the holy of holies,
        sketch out heresy,
                renounce sugar

while feeding on cream
      during reveille, take
            the bull by the horns.

This mourners' bench.
      Tossing and turning
            in this feather cathedral.

This bower devoid of attendants
      where you discover your rights
            and your wrongs.

This sacred calling that
      you leave forever
            with words unspoken, unknown.

*

This moon engraved
      on a folded sheet
            of fine vellum. A snake glides

under the barn. As you wash
      his sins away
            with relish and gusto.

As he soothes
      your vows
            and wakens your oaths.

This wish stone
        as you welcome
                each other as guest and host

for the full-bodied hush.
        This flotsam and jetsam—
                Monday through Sunday—

you are enskied
        in the mockingbird's
                indwelling song

as it concocts
        a soporific
                of wolves, apples,

and aftershave,
        gossip and flattery
                and all the daily

contradictions,
        salty and unmelodious—
                this scent bottle,

clouds of cosmos,
        mallow and iris
                and marigold—

this root cellar
       where you give birth
            to each other

over and over.
       This eel bed.
           This loch.

*

This stork's bed. This blue
       hotel bed in Greece,
           where you master

bird flight
       and horse under
           a canopy of stars

without reins.
       This backroom
           spectacle, these cervical

unmade beds. This furnace.
       Recuperated beds
           turned into pianos.

Shape note,
       hymnology,
           and musical comedy.

Sounding board
      and sound box
            to yodel and chant,

hurrah and bawl,
      tango on the humming top,
            this long-playing record.

Jarocho harp.
      Your childhood pillow,
            feathers falling:

organ loft,
      tabla of cloud skin. Weather wheel,
            weather deck,

on the right side starboard,
      on the left
            your old dresser,

six-sided parabolic gospel.
      This radiant square
            filled with the treasure

you plunder,
      parcel out,
            through the night,

fifty-fifty. This still,
    calm wellspring:
        a turtle rests in watercress.

*

Beds we flee from,
    take refuge in,
        say our prayers,

promise never again:
    refugee beds, boat beds,
        dirt cots and pallets,

stacked carpets. Mud. Sticks.
    This carved crib
        in the sunroom,

the scent of orange
    cake and a juniper-infused
        stew. The rose

of the child's pink lips
    on the nipple
        of the dog star

she eyes in
    the sky's garden.
        The eiderdown nests

in Siberian forests.
        Estuaries side by side,
                cheek by cheek,

jowl by jowl.
        The gondola.
            Fog.

These nomad beds
        on the open savanna,
                where you capture

and encage mirages,
        settle, each sexennial,
                reproduce an oasis.

Weigh stations
        where you practice
            rapture

in the sulphur-bottom
        whale you slumber
                inside. This night

school of passive
        resistance as the lion
                rises above you,

you open his mouth,
      climb in—you know
            that is the only way to live—

swallowed.
      Sun-cured, sunk
            in his magnificent nimbus.

*

The bed you ride
      alone. A sheriff
            in a gold fleece robe.

Hood.
      Duet.
            Saddle.

Giddyup.
      Giddyup.
            A cowboy's mess tent.

From this seed house
      you spread the clover
            by hand

or with a hand-cranked
      broadcaster,
            between windrows,

ruminate, forage,
                    let your mind wander,
                                     learn all about hay

and binding rope on this hay boat.
                    In this bed of practical
                                     advice. Mouth doctor.

Skin cop. Milkman.
                    Inventor of instruments.
                                     Eye doctor.

You see your body
                    repeat in the chandelier
                                     as you twin yourself

at every turn
                    just because he told you
                                     he likes double serpents.

The war in the heavens
                    and the one here on earth.
                                     In his bed:

leftover verbiage,
                    golden equinox gate,
                                     the five-eight beat

between the moon and Venus.
          Chasm. Rind. Animal eyes in light
                    fixtures. He played you

so well only charms
          came out of your mouth.
                    A lost psalm found—

*

This tideway
          you swim
                    through sea grass

and silvers, purple starfish,
          forgotten sigil,
                    water-born,

through riptides
          and streambeds and runnel,
                    this spill box—

over old keys
          and mistakes
                    and cufflinks,

over fen and down
          into the deep blue
                    winding and twisting,

over wetland
    and crustal plate,
        through basin and bin,

through eye mote
    and needle and clef,
        this astronomical expanse,

the compass always
    pointing henceforth,
        and up to now,

and long since.
    Coiled clockwise
        and counterclockwise,

the harmonic motion
    of ups and downs
        that takes you

though the labyrinth
    of the new-mown
        and the moss-grown.

Through hyssop and poplar
    and figs in Astoria—
        this prosody

of trees, roots
    in the lowest rings,
        mid-branch, this bed.

*

This boxing arena.
    This revival picnic.
        Where you say

you are free—
    but you are
        too busy to be free.

This greenhouse
    and celestial radio.
        This tent bed,

tethered to hive and wind—
    this June, July, and August.
        This jelly.

Jelly. Jelly.
    These vast narrows.
        This hidden room

where you are good
    at stealing dice
        and saying good night.

Where we want. What
            we want. To want. What
                        we want and what

we want to want.
            This museum bed
                        where you wander without him—

alley beds.
            Recycled beds.
                        Truth tables.

Rocking in the hull.
            This is my half
                        and this is your half—

the invisible line
            down the middle—
                        this stretch limo.

This limestone slab.
            This jury box and jukebox
                        you play that plays you:

G7, H3, O26.
            These dos and the don'ts
                        that you count off

when you're hot
        on the trail—suspect beds.
             Right and then

left past pastry shop,
        haze, and back alley.
             Fields of beds,

this place to flee from, correct
        the record. Take secrets
             to the grave. Place

to prosecute, to bring
        to justice, to try
             yourself at night.

This empty space beside you
        like a Cold War spy.
             This recessed niche

where you rub the handle
        of a gun or a letter opener,
        gorge

on crispy duck in bed.
      To be greased.
            To be degreased.

The common shape
      you form on
            the common prayer.

Shovel Flower: Self-Portrait

Under belly
Over exposed
Under world
Over soul

                so
   ul
                    so
      ul
                        so
   ul

Over sold
Under plots
Over achiever
Under pants
Over cast
Under dog
Over weaned
Under seen
Over ture

Sho
                vel
      me
                    Shov
   el
                you

44

Some call me
a tool. I'm more
accomplice
—contrivance—
you wrap your hands
around me when
you need to uncover
it or bury it. It's not,
you know, the in
and the out, more
the up and the down.

        Dig
it.
        Dig
it.
        Dig
it.

You've got to
use your body
if you want
to use me.

Hammer Flower: Self-Portrait

Drop it. Drop
it. *Drop*
it.

House Arrest

I confess to these feet
tethered to the earth,
pulled down by force

every time I jump or try
to fly. Like you, an old tree
sentenced us, keeps our wings

under lock and key
so we'll bicker with the birds
over scraps of weather

and the privilege to sing
or be seen. In the dark,
we scavenge midnight,

make chains out of stars
and bracelet shame.
My biggest crime, I could

not trust. I confess, I shut
myself off from the one
I needed and loved most.

I confess, I could not be
woken or accept myself
to the river's basin to be washed.

I'm dirty, scratching love notes
on the wall. Tonight, outside,
winter, subzero. Too cold

to snow. The neighbor
next door shooting phantom
deer with a handgun,

his beagle tied to a tree.
Over wooden bowls,
we count, we've become experts

at counting. When did we
make each other serial?
The keys froze in the ignition:

tonight the moon rises
from a ravine, a spice drawer
of pickled ferment to feast.

For us it's only surveillance:
under surveillance we interrogate
each other's mouths, pursue

every laugh and cry as they twist
and turn through our time,
as we investigate and ransack

our dog-rabbit-wolf shadows,
the half ones, the whole ones,
and cross-examine every intent,

put hidden taps to choice
appendages. In the basement,
we de-crimson our one last apple,

cut a tunnel through the core,
truss ourselves in aromatics,
climb in and out to the garden:

among the capable trees,
the not-degraded weeds,
the flowers released,

arrested in light, we stand
on strong enduring feet,
confess, captives of earth,

to the heart, aflame, the source—
across this iced plain—
the only material witness.

The Hoarder

It will always be my desert my
desert where I buried my first lie
and the wind my wind that I pack
and stuff my wind that spun me gold until
I became a Hercules missile my pond
leaves spinning gold the drowned antlers
glowing mine the speckled black trout
swimming under the house a field of
yellow trumpet chanterelles, that view
you can't have, all my views, the bowl
of soap shards we washed the antique
knives I could cut you with if you try
to take father swimming now out past
the horizon my horizon past the El Paso
smelter the plastic bulls on the empty
rum bottles. At the race track
in Juarez—open the gates and let
the dogs run—the gates always opening,
the dogs just about to run.

Done

First stop Sole Sensations on the Square
because I hear they have Birkenstocks
on sale and while we try on shoes,
you the men's and me women's, we
mull over and theorize about friends
past and present: the cajoler, the cure-all,
the higher authority, the always startled
and the always weary, the long lost,
recent acquaintances, all aspects of ourselves
we don't want to dwell on too long,
so instead conjure and tickle ourselves
with the lives of others.
                        And I tell you
I've been reading vintage etiquette books,
finding solace in the proper forms
of address and correct modes for grieving,
planning semiformal picnics I'll never have.
How it's been not even one season
since he said he was leaving, that he
was done.—I am done, he said.
And you say, Let's go to the new
antiques store, and we sit on an old
turquoise sofa under a cork chandelier
and I go on and on about him, about us,
in shameful ways, shaming him, but I can't
stop myself, I wanted to be more restrained
about it all—*The least said about it
the greater the dignity maintained*, Eleanor

Roosevelt says on endings in *Common Sense Etiquette*. And Emily Post: *One can not too strongly censure the unspeakable vulgarity of the woman. . . who confides the private details of her life.*

A woman under a display
of ceramics is telling the owner about
a recent medical procedure. She says, no pain,
just two little incisions. Snip snip, she says
and scissors the air with her right hand.
Why couldn't it all be just two little incisions,
one here and one there—I place my hand
on two parts of my body, one here
and one there and then all done.

Next over
for ice cream and I get a watermelon and lime
snow cone thinking it will taste as good as it did
long ago at dusty Saturday afternoon baseball
games, but it doesn't and then I say let's drive
out to the country, out to the barn and give
the horses a bath, sponge them down,
offer some relief from the humidity and flies,
and you say okay but that you have never been
on or around horses and don't know anything
about bathing them, that in fact they kind
of scare you, so I tell you not to worry, I'll
show you.

So when we get there, I tell
you to go to the barn and take all your
clothes off, to leave them there and then
meet me in the garden. That I'll show you
how it's done. I fill the big trough
with fresh cool water, collected
from big blue rain barrels. Careful,
careful now, don't get those new
Birkies wet.
                    I slip the halter on your head,
gently, not to hurt your ears or pinch
your neck. Then I wash you as if you
are a horse, scrubbing and brushing
you in long slow circular movements,
clockwise and counterclockwise,
sloughing and rinsing off the sweat
with suds of aloe and hyssop, until
you nuzzle my back, licking some
of the watermelon lime syrup off
my neck, you dig a shard of soap
into the ground with your hoof—
then I take off the halter—and then
we both take off, not into a field
or pasture but an opening—all
muscular opening—a threshold—without
flaw or blame or memory. Undone.

Duende

An hour inland from Bangor, Maine,
over rolling hills, in an oval pasture
surrounded by giant conifers,
the forest floor bejeweled
with ruby-studded mushrooms,
I watch the sheep sing,
if bleating could be called a song.
Maybe someone in a grove long ago
saw a man attached to a beast
of burden and so the concept
of the satyr was born. Memory is
the past reversed. I once
went out with a sailor, a Spaniard,
from Andalucía. We met at sea
where I worked the roulette wheel
in the ship's casino. His legs
were slightly bowed, his voice
gruff and torn, and when he came
the sound seemed to climb up
not from his throat but from his feet
smelling of earth and sea and grief—
a deep song Lorca called *duende*.
It wasn't pretty. His blue and red
and purple briefs soaking in a bucket
by the cabin door. He told me once
when he was a boy his grandmother
had caught him trying to fuck
a chicken. *The poor chicken*,
he laughed, his saddle-worn Andalucían

laugh, feathers flying everywhere, his
grandmother screaming. And what
to call those half-human, half-chicken
kinds of days: scratching and clawing
at the earth, bathed in dust,
trying not to think about the simmering
anise, peppercorn, and broth.
When I visited him, he met me
at the airport. Then the long train
ride south through field after field
of sunflowers. *Por la tarde* families
paraded, *por la noche*, only men
and boys and *extranjeras*—foreign women—
out past sunset. In an empty disco six
or seven guys danced, throwing themselves
around madly, slamming into each
other to Blondie's "Heart of Glass."
Franco had died a few years back.
From my window that night, a full moon,
shadows of the town square, the boarded-up
cathedral, a cat in heat, the smell
of blood oranges. In the morning
his grandmother, all in black,
asleep stooped in a chair outside
my door. Nearby the ruins of an ancient
Roman temple, goats on hind legs
eating the pale green leaves from olive trees.

Ditto

Exit breath, enter potato
salad. Enter blueberry sky—
a froth of cream-whipped
clouds. Exit: Happy Independence Day!
All day Mr. Magnificent and His Reptiles
on the AM dial. Meanwhile master
apple and cherry trees bless us,
begetters of fireworks, fill us
full spectrum. Listen my children,
with gregarious snort-song
marching quick time in the parade:
fifteen couples do it doggie style in quick time,
suck each other synchronized
and ditto and ditto and the whistle blows,
roman candles explode, chrysanthemums,
big colorful beach balls at the summer share
back and forth, forth and back,
the crack and slurp of clams
on the half shell, the ball slaps
into the catcher's mitt, the crowd goes wild, screams
his name over and over yes and yes. Pong
ping and ping pong repeat and send it back,
contagious fire after fire repeating bolt
action—the rifleman tosses the baton
twirler into the sky. She fires up a constellation. I
match you. And raise you. Toes matched. I miss you.
I miss you too. The fire-blue polish. The blue
negligee. 100 pony dolls at the Target
in cute outfits. Fits? Fits—

one size fits all. Ditto the stars,
ditto the moon. Ditto that day with you.
Oh can't we bring it back reproduced:
tenfold dittos, the tide pools full
of pulsing green anemone and giant purple starfish?
Ditto for me please the first time you kissed me,
stars like jacks cross the sky repeating,
blinking. You give it to me and I give it
back to you. Let's play catch, ditto me
and I ditto you. I love you sweetheart. I love you
too. Knock knock—the polished doorknob—
Who's there? Ditto. Ditto who? Ditto.
Ditto who? Ditto. Ditto who?

What Is Ohio? Who Is Mr. Ellington?

I can't remember his face, the deep furrow, his mix tape cassette—
though I know every note was marked with sanctity's odor and secrets.

The sun came out today (ta-dah!) with faint overtures of clarinet.
Grilled skewered beef, six-winged angel billiard hall, roiling heaven scent.

I want in. I want out. In out in out in out: O coquette.
Q: Hello? Mister Fist? A: My first rosette.

The Usage Panel finds *gavel* as a verb, with regret,
unacceptable. The soul creamed, dome of flies, spread out on ice dinette.

He visited me last night. My second bet.
A good bourbon, a crappy hotel room, the leverage of his turbojet.

I joined the trees last night: mean drunks, lashed tongues, slurred threat.
As the drunk angel falls, so a frothy uncorked lament.

Fuck fuck fuck or a polite old-fashioned perfumed sunset.
A polar bear walks into a bar and orders three rounds of arctic melt.

Young soldiers in flimsy coffins. Email subject line: don't forget.
Myrrh, thistle, wings, carbon net.

Please send our regrets, our nimble-stained-fingered public debt.
The heart bitten into a typeface called oubliette.

Thief, cleanse me with your purified sweat.
From the Midwest, CB sends corn casserole, big bands, alphabets.

The Convention

Tell her she needs to make a sunset
in the next five days. We've just got
two or three weeks to get the oceans
in place. Bottom line, who's on top
of the plateau? Plan the relevant scales,
hues, terrains, escarpment. After lunch
a core strategy for chasms and tides
must be identified. Do we still need the serpent,
that old ark, and the fig? The firmament
and the mist are no longer cost-effective.
We'll deconflict and degrade the horned
and the finned by seventy percent.
We may have to downsize *the human*.
The studies will examine benefits
following a chain of command—
Whene'er, wheresoe'er, whensoe'er—
A prayer flower releases boat-shaped
pods that sail aloft, releasing to the wind
an infinity of threads and seeds.

Sin Eater

We start off slow,
just a mote from the crock
redolent of bouts

of oil spill, evasion
pickled, a bubbling
daub of crooked

stocks deep-fried
with batter. Our napkin's
smeared crimson

with smothered salmon,
frogs, polar bears,
ducks, the thunder

of trees as they fall
in arctic winds now
gone south, rillettes

of shipwrecks, Pacific Rim
fleshpots deviled
in a garden-variety pickle,

fermenting in bonuses
for weeks. It's not hard
labor, eating debacle,

NFL tackle, little office
betrayals, lifer tears, a rub
of sniper, post-explosive

tremor of the drone
operator, food-waste
methane. We're not

finished. We never
finish—that's the best part,
the worst part: we never

finish. Full-time
devourers, hired
for our gut, our desire

to please, our teeth,
our ability to wipe
your plate clean.

Little Feasts

Loving you is like bread dipped in salt.
—Nazim Hikmet

Like juice of pickled lemons, serpent garlic, slow-cooked, spread on a bed of greens, packed in cheap coastal salt, stir-fried, stewed, seared, an aged soy sauce, a well-flavored stock, deep-fried with a tartar of malt vinegar, battered in brown ale, plain flour, and an egg, blocks of compressed tamarind, soaked and mashed, curried leftovers, caramelized, fried fish in salsa verde, wild fennel, parsley, étouffée smothered in its own juices, jack and pompano, mango and spring onion, coriander, lime leaves, ginger root, mackerel, clam hash, gulf coast gumbo for meatless Fridays, oyster beds, catfish in buttermilk and cornmeal, *mole negro*, almonds, ground cloves, cinnamon, savory pastries, skillet snapper, a rub of paprika and cayenne, bitter chicory, sweet orange, paella de campo eaten straight from the pan with the three fingers of the right hand.

Leftovers

Here's the bottle
opener you bought
at a flea market
in Beijing, a devil's face
with a big red shlong.
Here's the soap, shaped
like a giant green frog,
I washed you with. Here,
the little pinching tool
for pulling the stems off
new-picked spring strawberries.

II

The Frida Kahlo Tree: A Fable

She never felt so human,
the spring she turned into
a tree. How strange, at first,
pulling moisture up through
her roots that mirrored
her crown above, laden
among cones and blossoms,
entangled in butterfly and bee
rivulets—her skin a bark
for doctoring moss, her leaves
shimmering and spinning in the winds
with God's language. Wayfarers
and sailors rested in her hallow.
Her hundreds of mouths opened
and closed all at once, indoctrinating
all the elements save one.
         Then the darkness began,
the wrapping and braiding of her arms
by unseen hands or maybe
by her own, the tarred canvas
and crotch strap drawn tighter
at the throat. The staking of her tongues,
her branches grown into butcher knives.
She scoured the horizon for the sun:
her heart. All trees have hearts.
Her heart became a magnifying glass,
the burning mirror dilated—

the sun burned all the bindings
off, setting free her wandering selves.
Resin and smoke rose to the stars.
And sometimes after work or at home she senses
clusters of new blossoms on her boughs.

Thug Flower

arf arf gobble nip
a prefab golf iron
a prefab frog lion
a barrel of pro pig-no
a baffle groin fable fist

Twat Flower

flatter wow
frat rat wet
flow war felt
two waft trowel
fat welt row

Slit Flower

self writ lo
wife trolls
wells for it
slower lift
wolf liter
fowl tower

Thumbscrew Flower

belch few worms rut
clefts whom we burr
crows fumble throw
femurs wretch blow
Mr. Wolf we butchers

Suck Flower

sucks slog runt
cult gross sunk
crust slog sunk
suck lung trust
chattel gush gown
hatch set glow gun
latch-egg shut now
clash we thong gut

Gag Flower

Gag Gum Gnash Glog
Slum Gong Gang Gag
Gang Gash Gog Glum
Gang Slag Gogh Mug
Gang Shag Agog Glum
Gang Gal Go Smug

Dog Flower

Dog Flower is a stand-in
for the jukebox repairman.
He doesn't stand out,
but watch out, his panhandle
will bow your vocal cords.
Even when he's old
and has no appetite
Dog Flower will always
insist on the juiciest tender
bite of what's marbled
and spread out on the table.

Frog Flowers

Tell us the story again Papa
of men turned into frogs
for refusing to share their water.
No longer silent partners
with the upright. Challenged
in other ways to defend the pond.
Tell us, Uncle, if you can still
talk about the war in the desert,
how the desert wind blurred the men,
rendering them less than human,
wanting for nothing but water.

Dirty Aubade

Hard-pressed   foot-forward clouds   a man's full pour
of starless night   this ocean's strapless shoulders
that necessary affair with loneliness   his delivery
at dawn   making all the right routine stops
over body   over eyes   over West Texas vista
inner thighs   knows the full meaning
of elbow grease   on hands and knees
he scrubs down what's left of dawn   makes it shine
what's squeezed out of a no-name weed
oyster afterglow we raise to the gods   stained
and bottled-up memory unpasteurized and raw
river slough   tree clabber   milk wind
infuses the trees until they are rearing
like tethered horses—the bunting just now off the branch—
light over water—you get a taste for it
the sun rises up a purifying storm
as for love
our heads up to the sky
mouths wide open

The Stall

How we slept not on the open gravel,
but in the corner of the animal's stall.
That night the ghost of a great thoroughbred
kicked at our innards. We heard the great
animal chuff with delight, and when
it flopped on its belly you took me.
The moon made a lattice on our backs.
We were old, traveling far, walking from barn
to abandoned barn. One night we washed
in a trough of rain water and dreamed
a pig's dream: there in the sty aglow,
the savior we had been waiting for,
the starred eyes filled with light.

Hobo Flower

I shell rhapsody and rain
on each of the seven days
with nothing but a blade
of sun in my back pocket.

Story of a Tree

I loved this tree.
South of San Antonio,
west of the heart,
growing in the ravines
of the Pecos River
inside me, down across
the Rio Grande and up
into the Llano's staked plains,

tree of memory, tree of ghosts, tree of rain—

under birdsong whispers
you cradled me in your canopy.
When I was a baby, I stroked
the soft hair on your leaves.

You were my first true church,
and when rains came
our whole bodies shook
and shimmered with God's words.

You let me bury
all my secrets in your dirt
and sleep in your altar
as we drifted through stars.

Forgive me, Tree, for humiliating you.

I kicked at your bark. Spit on you.

Tree, I cut you
and carved cruel words
on you in reverse
in my rough, crooked cursive,
with a rusted green knife
I stole from a bitch,
scarring your sacred skin.

I burned you with a lighter
shaped like a cowboy boot,
left bird dogs tied to you
for days on end, let drill sergeants
in training from the nearby base
lash out and practice on you.

I let belly-gods, plug-ugly bruisers,
devouring cowboys and butchers
stuff themselves into me,
hog-tie me whole and slap me
around as you watched.

When I laughed and made
animal sounds, I scared you.
I chewed you out. Made fun of you.

I used toxins and poisons
to make you immaculate.
I wanted you perfect.

I nailed a no-trespassing sign
and a big security light to your side.
I sold pieces of you off.

I abandoned you.
I abandoned myself.

All around us the underground world overflows with love.

Season after season you return,
sap rising up from your roots,

unfinished, always becoming.

I defended against love

for as long as I could

until I couldn't.

You no longer have to hide your self in your deepest self.
You no longer need the ones you thought you most needed.

I know I am not good
at this, or anything really, but I'm trying.

Roll on, roll on, roll on—

Tonight, I'm wearing a red dress,
under a man's honeyed mouths and tent.

Your red flowers open and crown
and cover us in a Sunday of pollens.

And when I press my ear
to your thickness,
to your heart, I hear:
bells, bells, bells.

For the Lost Women in Prisons: A Texas Two-Step

She's hay poured
On a burning bed

She's an envelope
With a love letter missing

She's 4 a.m.   She's amen
She's chewing bone

She's the grease stain
On your grease-stained apron

She's forget-me-nots
Forgotten   She's a salt lick

She's so hot
They fried an egg in her head

She's a gas can
She's matches

She's just-picked
Cherries   She's a gag bit

A snaffle bit
She's the shuffle

In Texas two-step when he cut in
She's snake bit   a horned sidewinder

She's an erased route
She's a garden of mouths

She's the coastal duck's
Fine down stuffed

In your pillow   She's an old spice
Grinder   She's what's tied

To a hitching post   She's Pentecostal
Hymns 4 and 6   She's the rubbed-out sky

Blue Cadillac   Black as the casket
Grilled and married in mockingbird trill

She's the skinned
Armadillo boots

If you want her
Look for her under your bootsoles

She's sheared lamb infused
She's a rancher's blown glass

She's refracted   She cuts
The moon into a thousand slices

She's wild asparagus   a bait shop   She's spilt milk
She's refried beans   lost wallets   red chili   socket wrenches

Her name under rocks   under roots of river cypress
A child asks, what is the grass?

Across the range   She's the wind
Witch grass   love grass   wild rye

Your mouth on your lover's thigh
What has become of the women and children?

She's a mother's lost song
She's the gulf grass you lay down on

She's a cage of gassed canaries
She's the honeybee on your grave

Trick Flower

The mismatched girl sliced
up and stacked,

divided into three
matching cabinets, emerges

whole and unharmed, voilà,
from the bedroom and parking

garage, year after year. She knows
how to fit in. Now watch her float

like a cloud above the couch
every night after dinner. Not good

with zippers, she's an expert
when it comes to cranks,

churning and turning until
she's flat as a pancake.

With her head tight in a metal cage,
doves rise up in flight

from her pan of fire. A saw
illusionist, watch her cut herself

in half, then with a perfect cross-
stitch sew herself back together

with the seams invisible. Marvel
how she ties herself in knots.

Now restrainer, now restrainee,
she relishes changing places.

As a girl always in left field,
spaced out. She can catch

a bullet fired at her
direct with her teeth.

Tango (Cinema Sex Ed)

the come-hither glance   the head thrown back

the table dance   the predatory advance

the meal ticket out   the reclining on the couch

the pair of aces split   the feigned indifference

bikini and cape   the narrow escape

the billowy curtain   the ruggedly handsome

center stage   the expanse of her leg

surf crashing around them   on the edge of the bed

hot on the scent   they spin as one, the wheel of roulette

the manner to which she is accustomed   the object undetected

Little Pink Pouch Flower

I sewed a pouch out of a remnant
of pink terry cloth to keep the antique
lock that I gave you. The antique lock
with a small lever that revealed, when
you moved it with your finger, a hidden
opening. At its center a wellspring
brimming over with the bittersweet
and bosky inflorescence we soaked
in and swilled. Awash and drunk
you chased me over moss
and through night-blooming vines,
antlers aglow with animal
pleasure, night after starless night.

Backwater Love

Big, big, big, big, deepsome and boundless love.
Love that's all warp and sea expanse,
bulk love, sea bulk love: all splayed tonnage.

And love's oyster shell granulate,
scoured to a wizened spoon, just right to eat
the wind out of a salty morning. Love's remnants

and slag, lathe work barnacles knitted twice
over pilings. Love's museum of feathers:
barb, shaft, and filament shampooed

and groomed with a froth pomade. Love's heart,
an old corncob whittled into a forgotten harmonica,
glowing with three golden motes,

the rest gone to the belly of a kingfisher. Love's cunt
of flaxen sea straw—a cherry-bomb firecracker,
two broken crab traps, strewn into a crazy-quilt

alluvium. Love unfolds, giant blue stuffed
clouds with more clouds—uncrammed, clouds—
unhidden, clouds—uncrossed—perfect clouds,

ribbons of nothingness. Love's surface splattered—
all memory, a shell fragment. Love's trace—
an infinite and star-driven path.

III

Walking Stick

Tonight you guide me down
through the deserted horse farm
and up over the limestone quarry,
where we hunt for berries and morels,
under a full moon in a sacred grove
of felled elms. I rub nighttime
into your grain, admire the bowknots
of birdsong from Sundays past skewered
into your girth and paths.
How long it's been since I planted
mother's laughter and mother's tears
into your hardwood terrains
of rivers and caverns and canyons and dirt.
I hung Papa's old lures and the scales of angel
fish in your upper crevices. He always said,
Throw back the strange and beautiful ones,
they're poisonous. For a long time I thought
that meant he loved me less.
Now I see it was more a lesson on release.
In your crannies and chinks
I stashed Granny's crushed seeds,
mole poblano spice, her recipe

for *albondigas* carved down your side.
The mint and meat star-clusters whorled
in a golden broth jellied from whole roosters
she butchered in the backyard for supper,
while Tita chased Tootsie through
the breezeway with the entrails. I bound you
in mariachi chords, the red dress she wore,
the comb from her long red hair
as she sang *Volver, Volver.*
Her gold slipper sequins
hammered into your rough
with whisky emollients,
1000 eyes deluged and awash.
In your nave, a compress for bruises,
the black currant hammered
under her eyes and jaws,
Paw-Paw's hand-stitched deerskin gloves,
a Kiddush cup, remembered and kept,
and a lost man's ring from a plane
never salvaged. Walking Stick, my dog
licks at your wounds, pays homage
to the tree you never were

thieved from. A tree with blue jay nests
that had been spit on and hit
or loved and caressed by a wandering
stranger who slept and burrowed
in your center and dreamed
of a woman on a shore following
a horse never lost. Her amber eyes
and a rabbit he never caught
gleam from your caesuras. You are riven
with silver from the mines in Mexico,
salt from the salt swamps of Brittany,
and the salty fishing nets in Guaymas.
I garnished you with the molted lace
of snakes left under the corn,
poker advice and oyster-shell armor.
My father bearded with Bud Light and trident,
over a five-bushel burlap sack of oysters,
commanding a fiery ocean of molten
little oceans, as he stirred the coals
and frothy ashes, I was engulfed
in clouds of smoke. *Smoke follows beauty*,
he would always say. And I thought that meant

he loved me more. Now I wonder if he was saying
something about love and violence—a vision
of crops burning, houses aflame. He carried me
on his shoulders hunting white dove
in the cattle corrals at dawn in El Paso.
Here's the diamond cufflink stud I stole
from the devil and stuck in your middle.
At first, I thought he was a man:
under a Texas moon, we danced all night,
he taught me to whip and two-step
over tumbled quartz, tumbleweeds
and mesquite, Granddaddy's
metallurgies, along the banks of the Frio
strewn with the cow-bone piano keys
from the piano we tore to pieces.
And when the sun came up
I saw he had hooves instead of feet.
I wrapped them in a poultice
of torn music sheets and six broken
melodies. Walking Stick, you're shot
through and honeycombed with my first
and last lies, the smell of sex,

that abiding place in your corridors.
I belted you in hinterlands and backwoods.
In your secret hiding places I hid contraband,
secrets taken to the grave, serenades
from steel guitars, scored with a score
of sorrow-torn lullaby and hallelujah
sweat, dead doves crawling with ants.
On your stout end: cacti, dregs
and remnants, busted crucifixes,
rodeo belts and what's pickled.
In your blunt end: the silence of pecan groves,
the flashed silence of the burnt bodies
Hayden buried, after the bombings in Japan,
his shoelaces from Dallas ballrooms,
a cribbage board, and the threads
of my mother's embroidery—I'm singing
sana sana, colita de rana over her belly,
the grace that led my mother—amen—
down from that hill that day. Thank you,
Walking Stick, I fall easily. Over blue grass
and bogs, raccoon and possums
and cucumber magnolias, over

lacustrine wetlands and sediments,
the ghosts of the slaughtered embossed
in your bark segments, in your grooves,
braids, mirrors, and glyphs, through
your labyrinths, your chambers spun
with burnt El Paso lawns, lost children,
lighter flints and magnets, cottonwood
fluff and drive-in westerns, radio dials,
shotgun shells, lonesome whippoorwills,
bobby pins and iodine and coral lipstick.
The place I hid under the house
deciphering a mix of train whistle,
love and desert and the white spot
on the belly of a spider. Here on this night
where you teach me to walk gently
on the earth, and whole troubled times.
I swear by your guidance, leaving gifts
for animals, plants, and spirits
so they can heal or be unhealed.
You charm me across rope bridges
and lead me to what was never lost,

where the future becomes past.
Tonight under this full moon,
a dense tuft of fox hair
caught in a rose briar shines.
Here where I walk through my own night,
the night I offer to you as my own.
Walking Stick, where am I?
Grinding at the ground—
To go over a river where there is no river
and dream a dream I can't remember to dream.
To come on a cloudless night.
To reason with the wind on a path.
Smoke follows beauty, he said.

Alderman

Alderman, Lynette. She gave my goldfish artificial respiration. She lived alone with her father. He seemed very, very old and was never home. Maybe he was her grandfather, or uncle? She was six foot four. Or seven foot or eight foot or nine with gold hair to her waist. Her voice and laugh even bigger. She loved to go swimming in the Gulf during hurricane warnings. Lynette, where did you go? You disappeared. I suddenly remember men with shotguns trolling through the woods in August. Why do I remember them when I think of you? She would pick me up and lift me high over her head so I would not get smashed by waves. She was a giant.

Staychild

Staychild, Dallas. Surfer boy. Christian. A green bike he rode in slow S's. Fresh-picked blueberries and fresh trout. Gifts to my mother. We were swimming together at Deer Point when my brother fell off the pier. Where are you now, Dallas, with your blueberries and fresh trout?

Over to You

Back paths through cattails and grasses,
briar roses, the blue wolf dog foraging
in front. There he is again, 6 full moons
times 12, back racing after a ghost fox,
across the frozen lake, redefining silver,
as if in a fire heat to join the sacred pack.
A massive dog, he could climb a tree.
He broke into the smokehouse to eat
the stringed bresola when I was teaching
myself about smoked meats.

His body ferried in the fog to the north
shore through nebulae window. Does he live
in me again every time I cut a heart out and eat it?
His heart four times the size of a normal dog.
Sometimes I see him across distant plains.
He swam 25 miles along ranches and mesquite forest
and caves, in the spring-fed Frio.
We were in the world together.

Ahrooooooooo

Ahrooooooo

Aaahrrooooo

He was unknowable and yet he guarded
the unknowable part of me,
part of my dog self. Corralled in the den,

his ashes in a flowered box. At night
under a sky of stars, walking to a house
uncertain when he would come home
or sitting by the roots of the giant cypress.
Ready for a voyage at any moment
his memory confronts me.
And I ask you all to join me
for a howl at the eternal full moon.

Arhooooooooooo

Arhoooooooooooo

His canines, forked white spears.
His coat flecked with Baltic salt
and rare metals. His eyes,
pale yellow agates—his tongue
surreptitious, licking
salt quickly off a woman's
back legs and off babies' feet.
His father was a bear.
He was the giant of the litter.
He swam mighty currents.
Survived an ice break.
I have an eye for champions.

The Arrangement

At the annual summer writers'
conference, a group of men,
old friends, gathered for their annual
evening poker game. Among
the scent of lilac and the drone
of frogs at the nearby pond,
fireflies lazed up from the grass,
clusters of hydrangeas glowed
in the Vermont twilight. And one of them,
a writer, known for his Southern
style, his dirty realism, his shotgun
escapades, who had given up
his Shovelhead and drinking
a daily four fingers of charred oak mash,
sat at the table arranging wild flowers
with slow, meticulous precision.
You could see it made the other men
uncomfortable to watch their friend,
this writer known for his wild excess
and violence, caress each bud and petal
and woody stem with such tenderness,
tucking fronds and winding tendrils,
pollen stamens staining his fingers.
"Gelding," someone said. The dealer teased,
"Are you gay now or just mellowed?"
The men chuckled as they stacked
and counted poker chips. And the ante began:
mouths closed so as not to catch the smell
of breath, features blank to avoid

the tell. The flowers looked grotesque,
mocking, stuck in their aphrodisiacal
nomenclature, all spread open—
their unbearable fragility, their excruciating
brilliance revealed, exposed.

Let me tell you
that this weekend Sunday morning
the high-speed ferry pulls out
of Boston Harbor and my heart
opens—a favorite flower—and I love
how this full-blown pre-July
light splays and sequins out
into open sea. And I love these
Cape Cod potato chips. I eat
handfuls. Everyone's glowing.
Gulls swirl and dive, their
expletives made beautiful in
ocean whoosh. Sky scrubbed
down by salt spray to blue, bluer,
even more blue than all bluets.
All the best clouds out in Sunday
whites—snazzy! Muscular—
full-fledged—next to the sun
screen and flight plans I pull
out *James Schuyler Selected Poems*,
FSG. First edition. The only book
I brought with me. Joy.
Joy. Joy.—You signed off
in your letters: *Love, Jimmy*—
sometimes *Love, J.* I never
met you though I feel, formally,
of course, and with respect, you
are a constant, I mean, your poems,
read on patios, porches, trains—

various couches—the blue velvet
one, now, and that old secondhand
sectional—after one too many,
and in the morning with, yes,
poached eggs. And yes, now,
on the way to Provincetown,
MA, and I am surrounded
by gay men. Surrounded is
probably the wrong word. Sorry.
It's independence weekend.
The ship is full of muscle-bound
gay men on the outer decks,
lower decks, SRO upper decks: it is
a gorgeous day—gay men
in royal blue, bottle green,
and sailorly mustards flirt, play
cards, gay men in nautical-themed
tees, in matching tanks and shaved
heads. Two bodybuilders cuddle,
stroke matching amped-up
biceps. Gay men stare into identical
phones, magic mirrors, steamy
and jam-packed, a hothouse
of your flowers, James Schuyler—
the bruisers, the sinewy, the burly,
the beefy, the well-knit; in full force
polished: all fortified. A man
in orange trunks sits on a silver
metal box stenciled in orange:

6 CHILDREN'S LIFE JACKETS.
He looks like royalty stepping out
of an Italian painting or a lost
Long Island photo a half-century
ago. The overall mood is, well—
horny. And even the word *slacks* which is
not supposed to be pretty—it is pretty
hot here—I think they are back in fashion?
Were they ever out? Pressed, tight—
lemon, aquamarine, sunburned, toast—
Toast. You liked that word. And *blue towel.*
Slacks snug in all the right places—the men
check each other out. And that is a lot
of fun to watch. Refreshing. I wish
straight guys could look at each other
this way, I mean, at least, be more open
to admiring each other, their bodies
without all the violence of football, etc.,
in between. (at least I think I do.) Now
the clouds look like the Reddi-wip made
with real cream I have been drinking
with my French pressed coffee in the morning,
the press with the broken handle, since, well. . .
I don't want to go there now. Why?
Because I am here! The ocean
can be so healing, David says. *Ahem.*
French press. Almost everything, near
the ocean, is full of insinuation. Why
are the windows so wet? someone yells.

Explosions of laughter! See what I mean.
And then I imagine us all sinking down
and down—like a Pedro Almodóvar movie
mixed with an Esther Williams movie
and we all swirl in some kind
of slow-mo underwater choreography,
all the gay men and me, in the middle,
in my beach hat and giant green sunglasses
reading James Schuyler poems. No, I am not
a narcissist. I am, though, in fact
sitting, here, in the middle
of five guys, all revved up
and ready to party. They are on
their 3rd or 4th G & T and
they are comparing and critiquing
their Grindr profiles. (Would J.S.
and friends enjoy Grindr?) I am
rereading "Korean Mums" (are they
still called that?)—and trying not to look—
and to remember the first time
I read "Korean Mums," 23 years ago
now in the West Village. Down
the street from the French bistro
with the yellow geese sign. Is it
still there? At a party the other
day, I chose invisibility as my
superpower. Yikes. Where is my
sunscreen? And I have attempted
to write an imitation of the poem

to learn or embody the way it's so
light on its feet, shifting back and forth,
without effort from what seem to be
civilizing forces to innocent savagery. And
the guys in my booth are now talking about
the Manhunt Mansion, Team Bottom
at a recent scavenger hunt, lifting weights,
if and when to wear a jockstrap
at an underwear party—jockstrap? I text
Shannon back in Indiana. That means:
fuck me asap, he says. Oh. I guess
they are single, he says. The conversation
gets raunchier. And I guess
this could just as well be a straight
frat party except these guys are talking
about turning 34 and if they will be
seen as bears or daddies or twinks
(twinks? I text Shannon). I'm twenty
years older, and wonder how I'll be seen?
Traveling alone this year. And the guy
next to me plays the clown, when two
über-masculine guys walk by with twin
Weimaraners; he winks: *We'll break 'em*—
cracking up his friends. He moonlights
as a stripper, I learn, full of bravado,
with pale blue eyes like pearls or raindrops
over a tender meadow. He deserves his own
poem. *You can love someone and let
someone love you back,* Penny Arcade

will say at a reading a few nights later.
And I think of him. And no one is talking
about Fairfield Porter or *Middlemarch*. And
no one is wearing polka-dot scooter
skirts with lilac rings. Just ahead, Race Point
and Herring Cove come into view. The dunes
and marshland grasses look like the jacket
painting on your book by Darragh Park.
The ferry pulls up to the pier. The surface
of the water, a test sheet a watercolorist
uses on the edge of a painting to
work out the relationship of color to light.
See you at the tea dance! They wave
goodbye. I imagine you here, great poet,
joining the procession of men, your friends,
a few families, children and women,
into the Adamic salt air and the sky:
a cordial. We all drink it in—
together. Cordial, from the word
for heart. Someone yells *Trevor!*—
Note the light: all is possibility,
past and present merge. Today welcomes
the annual Portuguese Festival, Blessing
of the Fleet. Blessings to you, wherever
you are, Darling. When I come home
I promise that I will let you see me.
Once I took the *Collected Nietzsche*
on a trip to Cancun. That's how
much fun I can be on holiday.

June 6, 2015

For two days in June in the year of the goat,
we were nothing and everything,
dancing pianos, an afternoon choreography,
our mouths two harbors for canasta boats,
full of smuggled-in *mole* by the world's
shyest man. We were zithery banduras
and hot Bowery bards, we were Puma's
eyeliner, the school of hard knocks,
the very best lox, bath product confection,
pau d'arco and burdock protection,
and four little songs about lack from a poet
with an intense relationship with death.
We were long-distance texts from atlas
to bed, longitude 37, latitude "Come on in!"
We were walrus tusks and musky star anise
stuffed duck a-spinning. Alas, we were
a revelation of entrances of exits across
a cribbage board, we were polar bears
at dawn guarding the shore, we were tickled
whale fins, a poem in your book, Touré
on the radio, we were a creamy heaven
of Ample Hill crack caramel, a brisket taco hot
off the grill, we were the haunted horse
on the horsehair fiddle, we were the forest
reforested with millions of trees. We were ram,
wood goat, lamb. We were June. For two days.

Margarita

The gold sunburst over the Zenith,
where my first crush spun on vinyl,
Dean Martin. The minotaur in blue
gravel danced with an undulating couch.
A plate of oil-soaked napkins from deep-
fried tortillas. Flies all over the screen
porch door. And every year or every
few months, a different maid.
My father loved Carmen's enchiladas.
Why did Margarita get to sleep
with my little brother? The sunburn
line on my mother's back.
Where are you now, Carmen?
Margarita? Where did you go?
Ants crawling through the labyrinth
of the dead dove out back.

Rooster Skewers

Father smaller and smaller swimming
out to the second sandbar. The Gulf
of Mexico water shimmers with each diamond
stud I've lost. And Val and Mel's
shenanigans with my boyfriend
in that crusty condo shower. On the drive
back to San Antonio posing nude
on oil jacks. Delivering key lime pie
from my '38 Ford truck. There are only two
rooster-carved cocktail skewers of Mexican silver
left in the silver box. Along the way, a sunrise, that beaded
red dress. It went the way of an uncle's
collection of cockfighting blades. A child
in the making. A redhead maybe.

Dirty Hippie

Everyone is feeling virtuous this Saturday
morning. There's that periwinkle-eyed farmer
in overalls who has a genital-piercing business
on the side. It's raspberry season, and we sit
in the grass and listen to the all-girl doo-wop band
sing off-key. Earlier this morning I found
a dead mouse in a paper towel roll
behind the clematis vine bulging with purple
flowers. I stroke your cheeks with the delicate
anise fennel fronds. The clouds above
are white duck feathers in a snow-laden China
forest a century away. The past slowly
arrives into the present. *You may never get to*
have that conversation, you tell me as we stop
at the soap maker's table, smelling one
rendered with lard, patchouli, and lavender
called "Dirty Hippie." I buy two bars for Bob,
who is living in a yurt finishing his story
collection. The local restaurants are setting up
their booths in the parking lot, I am sorry,
as much as I love brisket I will not eat
brisket from a soggy paper plate standing up
in a burning asphalt parking lot. There is a
long line at the booth for fried mac and cheese.
I feel lonely for Texas or New York or anywhere.
Later tonight fireflies in a metropolis over the orchard
grass. Slices of fennel and cucumber.
A conversation we will never have.

The Revenant

When the track opened up he showed up: trained
in large animals and metal, with a gift for conjuring
risk and omission. The first day of racing season,
Mother and I standing at the stove
arguing as usual over just the right
way to make enchiladas and red chili stew when he walked

in on us. The bougainvillea robed over the walk,
purple and majestic, the bracts hard-trained
along a warped trellis, grown from a cutting he stole right
off the nursery's discount rack, branches strong enough to conjure
crucifixion. *Man alive, you two still at the stove*
fighting over enchiladas and stew? Mother looked at me with both seasons

in her eyes, rainy and dry, her divided way of seeing his seasonal
arrival, how he always asks the same question, how he walks
in as if he'd just gone outside for a smoke. Mother and I at the stove,
each with our own cast iron, never knew what car or train,
over how many epics, through which narrows, what conjugations,
brought back this man, who hired himself out for the right

half price: with a know-how for wildness. His right
hand stained by a destructive distillation, seasoned
now to an oaken finish, raptor-like, veined rivulets. His mouth a conjurer's
rabbit, risky and restless with a new trick to play on me. His walk
wound tight, watchful, a bark in a hound's mouth, a hound trained
to keep one eye on the wager and one on the stove.

Why do I think of a missing ingredient when he smiles at me? The stove
with a secret cabinet, mother bought it right
off the street from Mr. Yancey before he took to riding trains
and became a hobo jungle barber. What seasonings
we wrangled over, cayenne, arbols and amens, cuts of pork I had to walk
to town for. Mother wondering aloud if it wasn't the conjecture

of bickerings, the fomentations, the rub that conned
him back to us. Do you wonder when standing at the stove
or lying in bed or going out for a walk
how you'll act when the one who left comes back? No one right
way to say goodbye. Townsfolk say on the first night of racing season
you can see three ghosts at our ruined house past the train

trestle. Eighty years ago Mother and I walked beyond the train track.
We bought a stave of yew from the hobo barber, then conjured up a stew
and killed him, in full agreement over the seasoning. And we were hanged.

Sunday To Do

Wait for him by the fence, in nothing but a gallery
of ravenous. Place one silver dollar on the back
burner, cook up a salve, bless the morning thunderstorm,
her natty blue clouds making a mess. In your mind
mispronounce all the p's and q's until they reek,
note the ensemble of blue flowers, how chic to limit
themselves to one basic color. Make a big fuss
over the sky. Follow any old woodland path
to the old graveyard, note the gallery of forgotten
names: Zeporiah, Clement, Quintero, Rainwater,
Cenoiva Rapp, beloved wife of Isaiah. Remember
the tiny plot of abandoned military baby graves.
Mrs. Stringham, blue-suited, garlic-breathed,
instructing our troop on how to mind the neglected
tombs: scrub moss, plant flowers. Distillate
the scent of dying ferns. Gain a seat in the apple orchard
to watch the crows' cause célèbre. Bless the mystical
Hanoverian grazing on rain-glazed clover and dandelion,
saved from last April's kill auction. Ask the rain
for a rain check. Put mind to sky's long slow braise:
dirtblue figblue meatblue goatclouds cloudtongues
follow long bluuuueeee cloud threads unraveling
a growlery of French leonine clouds. My blue
heeler, blue-black ears. Dead now, a blue eon.
Remember walking in the rain on Ave. of Genies,
where it's always raining. Galleries of endless Egyptian
tombs at the Louvre. I miss my dog. Bless the ballot
of stars tonight, legal or illegal. Plant twelve blue
stars. So they will return to the hives, when the bees follow

be sure to tell them of war casualties. Tell them
a story about an old pair of boots. Big blue rain-
drops, blue blue blue drops on coffin tops. Mend
the cavern doors. Create a gallery of dream flowers.
Start with B: blue mindsets, bituminous blessyvines,
brooding fellows' breeches, blabbermouths (bloom when raining),
breast buds, bite gallerias, night-blooming broncos. Plant them!

Acknowledgments

Many of these poems first appeared in the following publications:

Black Renaissance Noire, Crab Orchard Review, Floating Wolf Quarterly Chapbook Series, The Harvard Review, Poets.org, The New Yorker, Sou'wester

Catherine Bowman was born in El Paso, Texas, and is the author of *1-800-HOT-RIBS*, reprinted in Carnegie Mellon Classic Contemporary Series; *Rock Farm*; *Notarikon*; *The Plath Cabinet* and editor of *Word of Mouth: Poems Featured on NPR's* All Things Considered. Her poems have been selected for several editions of the *Best American Poetry* series and have appeared in *The New Yorker, The Paris Review, The Kenyon Review, The L.A. Times, Ploughshares, Black Renassiance Noire,* and other journals and magazines. She lives on a farm and wildlife refuge in Bloomington, Indiana. She has taught in the New York City public schools and directed the MFA Creative Writing Program at Indiana University, where she currently teaches.

Publication of this book was made possible by grants and donations.

We are also grateful to those individuals who participated in our 2015 Build a Book Program. They are:

Jan Bender-Zanoni, Betsy Bonner, Deirdre Brill, Carla & Stephen Carlson, Liza Charlesworth, Catherine Degraw & Michael Connor, Greg Egan, Martha Webster & Robert Fuentes, Anthony Guetti, Hermann Hesse, Deming Holleran, Joy Jones, Katie Childs & Josh Kalscheur, Michelle King, David Lee, Howard Levy, Jillian Lewis, Juliana Lewis, Owen Lewis, Alice St. Claire Long & David Long, Catherine McArthur, Nathan McClain, Carolyn Murdoch, Tracey Orick, Kathleen Ossip, Eileen Pollack, Barbara Preminger, Vinode Ramgopal, Roni Schotter, Soraya Shalforoosh, Marjorie & Lew Tesser, David Tze, Abby Wender, and Leah Nanako Winkler.